BRODIE'S JOURNEY

WITH HOPE

How a diagnosis of epilepsy saved my dog's life

Hope Anderson

Burkwood Publishing Services
P O Box 1772
Albemarle, NC 28001-5704
www.burkwoodmedia.com

Printed in the United States of America

DISCLAIMER

Any comments or knowledge shared in this book regarding epilepsy treatments and protocols are specific to my experience. Seizure symptoms and activity will vary from one dog to another. Talk to a veterinarian or a veterinarian neurologist about your dog's diagnosis and treatment.

Dedication

To all the dogs who suffered with epilepsy and lost the fight … you are not forgotten.

To those dogs fighting to live with epilepsy… you are truly "epi" warriors.

To all the families of these "epi" warriors …you are not alone. *

* (See the Resource page for more information regarding online forums and groups that provide emotional and practical support for your journey).

Prologue

The morning of March 11, 2014, began like any other Saturday morning. Rise at 7:30am, start the coffee, let the dog out, etc. The day was overcast, but not raining, which was fortunate considering what happened next. I looked out the sliding back door to check on Brodie, my almost 7-year-old Border Collie mix. To my surprise, he was lying in the natural area of the backyard on his back, with his legs kicking up into the air in all directions! With a puzzled look on my face, I started out the door. My first thought was he was scratching his back, but it turned out to be something more serious. Within seconds, it was obvious something was very wrong. In a panic, I immediately ran out to him. His jaw was clamped shut; all the muscles in his face were contracted, leaving him with a grimaced look. I didn't know if he was in pain, but saliva was drooling from his lips. His legs were no longer thrashing. They had gone rigid. It frightened me, but I knew I had to keep my wits about me so I could help him.

Bending down next to him, I started talking to him and rubbing his back, being careful to stay away from his head. Gradually, his body relaxed, and he turned toward the sound of my voice; but could tell from the vacant look in his eyes he didn't recognize me. That was truly alarming. Slowly, he got to his feet, but looked dazed and confused. He stumbled several times as he attempted to walk. I knew with certainty he had just experienced his first grand mal seizure. In another couple of minutes, his face relaxed, and he started whimpering, as if excited to see me. Relief washed over me, glad that he was returning to his normal self. After his legs regained strength, we walked back to the house. Once inside, he continued to walk and pace. I just wanted to sit down and cry, but didn't. Instead, I walked along with him to prevent him from bumping into furniture or falling down. He let me know he was hungry, as he kept going to the cabinet that held his food; but being able to drink water first with no issues was my concern before feeding him. I soon learned that the seizure itself was part one; part two was this post-ictal phase, characterized by frantic pacing and extreme hunger. Eventually, Brodie settled down and began resting quietly. That's when I sat down and let the tears flow. Anxiety and disappointment washed over me, and heavy sadness settled into my heart. I had known this might happen, but had hoped it would not. Now that it has.... am I equipped to deal with this journey and all it will bring?

CHAPTER ONE

Trust in him at all times. (KJV)

~ Psalms 62:8a

Brodie and I began our life together in August 2007. I previously owned three dogs, one at a time, all female Golden Retrievers. Each one had a unique personality, and I enjoyed my time with them. Being single, my dog is my family-my best friend. The love and companionship from that bond goes deep with me. Sadly, the last 'Golden girl' departed tragically, and it took a long time before I was ready to try again. When the time came to move forward, I knew my choice had to be something other than a female Golden Retriever. That breed will always be my first love, but it was time for a change. My niece convinced me to visit her friend, who was looking to find homes for some puppies. I was a little unsure, but went..... just to look, of course. Several breeds were represented in the mixed group: Golden Retriever, Basset Hound, and Border Collie, to name a few. We delighted in playing with all the pups and had a variety of sizes and colors from which to consider. My niece chose a female, black with tan markings and a low body similar to a Basset Hound. She was named Bella. Instantly, I was drawn to a puppy that had black and white coloring and resembled a Border Collie. He was confident and independent; he was the one for me. A few days later, I brought him home and named him Brodie. He was twelve weeks old and full of energy. Every day was a new adventure. The crate training went smoothly, and it was clear he had a sharp Border Collie mind. Brodie was a star student at obedience training, but he had the advantage of being a little older than the rest of his class. He loved to run in the backyard, and it was apparent he had great herding skills. He loved chasing squirrels, but thankfully never caught one; they always escaped up a tree or hopped onto the fence. On his first visit to the animal clinic, my vet of many years remarked, "if you wanted a change from a female Golden Retriever, I'd say a male mixed breed is about as different as you can get."

A genuine statement; and the new beginning I needed. It thrilled me to be a "dog mom" again! Brodie had a normal puppyhood; he enjoyed playing with other dogs and spent time with Bella and the other family dogs.

Brodie and I made many fun memories during our first year together. In October we went to a fall festival and entered a contest…I've forgotten the category, but we had fun just being there together!

All the winter holidays were more enjoyable because of him. He received lots of toys that Christmas, of course, and in early 2008 he experienced his first snow. He loved it! I laughed at how he would run circles in the snow and bite it. If it was all snow, he enjoyed it; but if there was any ice or sleet mixed in, he wasn't as interested.

The next few years were normal. Brodie and I had many happy days and adventures. He grew into a nice, medium-sized dog, weighing about 35 pounds.

Then a disturbing thing happened. My niece's dog, Bella, had her first seizure in June 2013. It was a short one, but definitely a grand mal. I hated it happened to Bella, and it gave me great concern for Brodie. While Bella and Brodie didn't look anything alike, they had the same genetics. Now I lived with the dreaded realization a seizure likely would happen to Brodie as well. We had another eight months with no incidence. The expectation of "waiting for the other shoe to drop" was oppressive, but I watched him closely. Then the monster struck. Brodie's first seizure was on a Saturday morning in March 2014. His life–and mine– had forever changed.

CHAPTER TWO

Get wisdom, get understanding: forget it not.

~Proverbs 4:5

Obviously, my next course of action was to visit the vet and get more information. My local vet examined Brodie and ordered a blood panel to determine if all his bodily levels and functions were normal. She also asked if Brodie had been recently exposed to any odors, new shampoo, different food or treats, etc., that could have triggered a seizure. I didn't recall anything new he had been exposed to, and his blood work was normal. After ruling out these metabolic and environmental factors, the vet diagnosed Brodie with idiopathic epilepsy. Great, I have a diagnosis.... but what does that mean? Can seizures be prevented? Is there a treatment or medication that will control or stop the seizures? To be honest, I left with more questions than answers. My face still reflected as much concern as when I walked in, and the fear in the pit of my stomach was hanging on. I came home and dove into online research about epilepsy in dogs. Between that source and my vet, the answers were there is no "test" for epilepsy. Veterinarians reach the diagnosis by eliminating all other possible reasons or conditions. They do not introduce seizure medication until seizures become more frequent or severe. This is more than one a month or two in twenty-four hours. This knowledge just left me feeling frustrated and helpless. I realized there was no easy fix or cure; but what I could do was learn how to help Brodie through a seizure, and know the danger signs if urgent medical attention is required. Believe me, seizures are frightening to witness. It's very difficult to watch your pet experience one, but you have to keep calm and focus on what you can do to help. Their life depends on you. Preventing your dog from injuring itself is critical, timing the duration of a seizure is important, and rescue medications have to be given–all at once. It's like juggling balls in the air, hoping you don't drop any, especially if you don't have anyone else in your household to assist. Did I mention ice? Placing an ice pack on the dog's lower spine can keep the body temperature from getting too high. The other benefit of icing is it helps shorten the seizure time and the recovery time. As a single dog mom, I never had time to get an ice pack from the freezer. I couldn't leave Brodie unattended. Timing the seizure is important, as the longer it lasts, the higher the body temperature rises; and an extremely high temperature or a seizure that lasts over four minutes might cause brain damage. Seek immediate treatment at your vet or emergency vet if a seizure goes on too long.

CHAPTER THREE

The Lord is my strength and my shield.

~Psalms 28:7

Brodie settled into a seizure pattern of one about every three months. Every time the calendar would begin approaching the eighty to ninety-day mark, I became anxious. You know a seizure is coming and you dread it, but there's no stopping it; you hope it is short. His second seizure was on July 6, 2014, again, early in the morning. Much like the first one, it was a grand mal seizure, very frightening, but thankfully only lasted about one and a half minutes. The third one came on October 18, 2014, similar to the others. I was always glad to get through the dangers of the actual seizure, but dreaded the post seizure phase almost as much. During a seizure, dogs lose their motor skills, become temporarily blind and disoriented. Even when the seizure stops and your dog attempts to stand, he can stumble and fall, will often pace continually, and become extremely hungry. Brodie's pacing usually lasted about thirty to forty-five minutes, but some dogs go longer.

I would walk around with him, bending over him to prevent him from running into furniture or door jams. That was uncomfortable for my back, but it helped him, so I always stayed close. Brodie also desperately wanted to eat. The extreme hunger is from the seizure depleting the glucose in the blood. The challenge was to hold him off until I knew he could safely swallow. Water was always offered first and if he could drink and swallow, then small amounts of food. I knew if I gave him food too soon, he would likely throw up, which might put him into another seizure. When Brodie finally would calm down and be ready to rest or sleep, I was relieved and exhausted; but I remained on alert. I would continue to watch him for a while to be sure he was completely settled. When the brain gets scrambled, it can take a while for it and other body functions to return to normal. If you think of the brain as an electrical box, then a seizure is like a blown fuse that has to be reset. The only fortunate thing about this, based on what veterinarians have told me, is that your dog does not experience any pain while in a seizure. Since their brain is not functioning properly, it cannot register pain. That is good to know; but it didn't help me with my pain and heartache for Brodie, that he has to live with epilepsy. It was also during the next few months that I noticed something else was happening. Brodie experienced what appeared to be a 'fainting' spell of some sort. This was evident if he had been running very fast and then would stop, start stumbling and nearly fall down. In November and again in December, this occurred; and when explaining it to the vet, I was told it could be a type of seizure known as a focal seizure; but these often include head tremors, licking lips, fast eye blinking, etc. I didn't recall seeing Brodie doing any of those behaviors during his episodes. On January 24, 2015, he had his fourth grand mal seizure, similar to the earlier ones. At least they were remaining relatively short. He also continued to have episodes of 'fainting' in March and early April, once while family visited. We were in the backyard, letting him and the other family dogs play. Brodie was very excited and running a lot. When he looked like he was going to fall over, my brother-in-law stopped him from running. In fact, I made Brodie come inside and rest. Then, about two days later, April 8, 2015, he had another grand mal seizure. This was the first time a seizure happened during the middle of the night, around 3am. Can you imagine waking from a sound sleep because your dog has started thrashing violently? After two minutes passed, the thrashing stopped; but after twenty seconds or so, he started thrashing again for another fifteen to twenty seconds. This had not happened before, but the second one ended quickly. It made me concerned about how this seizure was different, but he quieted down and I went on to work. When I got home about six pm, Brodie seemed to be his usual self, so he went with me to my sister's for supper. About 8:30pm we were sitting in the living room talking, and Brodie was lying in the middle of the floor. Then we heard movement and realized he had walked behind the chair I was sitting in and was having another seizure. Since this was not the usual pattern, I decided we would stay at my sister's overnight, should we need help. I quickly went back to my house, about fifteen minutes away, to get a few things. Before my return, my sister called to say Brodie had experienced another seizure. When I arrived at her house, I put Brodie in the car and drove to the emergency vet. This was his first time of "clustering" that is, having one seizure without fully coming out of it, and going into another one; or when two or more seizures happen within a 24-hour period. When we arrived at the emergency vet, they immediately took Brodie back for examination. By this time it was nearly 11pm or later. Truthfully, I had lost track of time. I sat in the waiting room, feeling anxious. The room was quiet, but that only let my thoughts run wild. Would Brodie pull through? Why are the seizures escalating? After what seemed a long time, the vet met with me and said Brodie would have to stay overnight. They had started the first of four bags of IV Phenobarbital, a 'loading dose' to calm his brain, and get the medicine quickly into his system. The next day, he would begin Phenobarbital tablets for seizure management. My vet explained the goal in treating epilepsy is to keep seizures from happening very often and to be of short duration when they do. "Why can't we aim for not having any?" I asked, but was told that is uncommon. I just wanted to keep Brodie from having to endure these seizures! Still, I was glad that Brodie would now be on medication going forward, and hoped it would lessen the frequency and duration of his seizures.

Treating epilepsy is a trial-and-error process. Initial medication is introduced, which works for a while, but often a break-through seizure happens. Then, the doctor increases the dosage of the medication and/or introduces another one. The goal is to find the right combination of medication that provides controlled seizure management, which is easier said than done. A lot of the medications have side effects and you see your dog become a walking zombie for a while, or show other behaviors not normal for them. It's a heartbreaking and frustrating pattern. Despite your best efforts to give medications daily and on time, control for environmental conditions, feed a proper diet, etc., a seizure can randomly happen; and as a 'parent' you feel like a failure. Living with epilepsy is like riding a roller coaster. There are highs and lows, and unexpected turns.

CHAPTER FOUR

For I the Lord thy God will hold thy right hand, saying unto thee
Fear not, I will help thee. ~ Isaiah 41:13

Brodie began medication on April 10, 2015, and adapted to it easily. Our new schedule included him getting Phenobarbital pills at 6:30am and 6:30pm. His blood was regularly checked to ensure the medication was providing a therapeutic coverage, and that he had no side effects. In between his seizures, Brodie was perfectly fine. He, like many dogs, lived a normal life despite his disease. However, his pattern was definitely changing. Even with the medication, Brodie had another seizure a month later, in May, and then another on June 23, 2015. Bro, this is not what we want to happen! Both times, the seizures were only a minute or so, but happened in the evening while he was resting or sleeping. How can the brain go from being calm, or so I presumed, to being in a full-blown seizure? It seems that during sleep the brain is still active; therefore, the potential is there for signals to "miss-fire" and cause a seizure. There were many evenings I would go to bed dressed in casual or comfortable clothes, in case we had to leave during the night for a trip to the vet. Unfortunately, his pattern was getting more frequent, which was not the right direction. Bloodwork was repeated to check the Phenobarbital levels, and the vet increased Brodie's medication dose. They added a rescue medicine (liquid Valium), which he would receive immediately after a seizure to calm his brain faster and prevent secondary seizures. It is essential to have a rescue medicine and protocol in place as part of seizure management. The liquid medication is given by inserting a syringe up the dog's nostrils-easier said than done, of course, but I learned quickly. We got through July without Brodie seizing; but the next episode came in August, one so horrific I thought I was going to lose him.

On August 5, 2015, in the early morning, Brodie had a seizure. It was normal, although I noticed the confused and wobbly state did not last very long; he went fairly quickly into the pacing and excited "feed me" stage. Still, he settled down and the rest of the day was uneventful. That all changed around 9pm that evening. He had a major seizure;

it lasted about the usual one to two minutes. At 9:20pm, he had another seizure, much like the first. Horribly, he had a third seizure at 9:40pm and actually got vocal during this one, barking and yelping, while lying on the bathroom floor. The barking…. it broke my heart to hear it; he'd not done that ever before. I knew it didn't mean he was in pain, but it was still very upsetting to witness. The seizures were so close together, he didn't stop thrashing in between them; I could not get the liquid medicine up his nose. I was beside myself…trying not to panic, trying to watch him and talking on the phone with the emergency vet. Knowing I needed a ride to the vet, as I could not watch Brodie and drive at the same time, I called my brother-in-law to drive Brodie and me to the emergency vet. Before my ride came, I tried one more time to insert the liquid valium up Brodie's nostrils, but failed. In desperation, after the third seizure, I squirted the medicine down his throat, hoping he would swallow and get it in his bloodstream. After the last seizure, he continued to bark, though his body had stopped thrashing. He barked so much he made himself hoarse. He was still barking and groaning when we arrived at the veterinarian's office. Sitting in the back seat with Brodie while my brother-in-law drove, I began thinking, is this the end for Brodie? I was terrified. I kept praying to God, "don't let this be the end of him, please save him." The veterinary team met us in the parking lot with a stretcher and took him straight back to begin treatment. They kept him until the next day, giving him 4 bags of IV Phenobarbital overnight. The next day, when I picked him up, he was a little unsteady but had gotten through the danger zone. The decision was made to increase his Phenobarbital medicine and add a second medication, Zonisamide. We had survived a very serious cluster seizure, but it was still uncertain about how quickly the increased medications would help. In fact, over the next several days, Brodie continued to have occasional episodes of focal seizures. It was obvious that his brain was not settling down. I even took him back to my vet so they could watch him while I was at work. Some episodes he had at the vet clinic also included not just his head bobbing, but his shoulders shaking, too. It seemed best to leave Brodie at the vet another day or two for monitoring. I checked on him daily; they would bring him from the hospital side into an exam room so we could visit.

The vet recommended referring us to the neurologist at the local specialty veterinary clinic. It would take a few days to schedule the neurologist appointment, so I decided to leave Brodie at the local vet as he continued to have little head bobs and tremors during his stay. Desperate for answers, I was more than ready to get Brodie in with a neurologist. By this point, I had many questions going through my head. Will we get the seizures under control and back to a manageable frequency? How long would it take? Or even worse thoughts, such as, is this just truly epilepsy? What if there is something wrong with his brain? Were the seizures possibly from a tumor or lesion in his brain? I wasn't sure if I could continue with the assumption that all this was epilepsy. If it was not epilepsy, what would happen next? What other organ or system in his body would start to fail if his brain continued to deteriorate? Would changes in his brain lead to any abnormal aggression? Would Brodie take longer and longer to recognize me after a seizure? Let's face it, when the brain is jumbled, it's hard to know what to expect.

I made the decision that I had to know if this was truly epilepsy, or if something different was happening in his brain. This would require an MRI, so the primary vet sent a referral to the local neurology specialist. I hoped that pursuing this option would provide answers to some of my questions. Little did I know just how much was about to be discovered…and none of it was good.

CHAPTER FIVE

He shall call upon me and I will answer him, I will be with him in trouble. ~Psalms 91:15

On August 12, 2015, I picked up Brodie from my vet and drove him to the specialty vet hospital to meet with the neurologist. He explained the procedure for the MRI, and took Brodie to the back for an initial exam and prepare for the MRI procedure (which is done under anesthesia). I waited in the lobby for a brief period, but believed it would take another hour before they provided me with an update. My phone rang as soon as I went to the café across the street to grab lunch. It was the neurologist, with some disturbing news. When he began to administer the anesthesia, Brodie's heart rate plummeted. Brodie's heart rate dropped dangerously low when the anesthesia was administered. Even though drugs were given several times to stabilize it, it only remained stable when the anesthesia was discontinued. The vet said he had to withdraw from attempting the MRI, as he would not put Brodie at risk. With the elimination of the MRI, the neurologist handed

Brodie over to the cardiologist to examine Brodie's heart and determine what had caused the heart rate to drop so severely. The rest of this day changed from "what is wrong with Brodie's brain?" to "what is wrong with Brodie's heart?" For the next several hours, the cardiologist did extensive testing on Brodie: an ultrasound of his heart, an EKG, and even an ultrasound of his abdomen, to rule out any underlying gastro-intestinal issues that could be affecting the heart. The cardiologist reported that Brodie's condition was a 'high grade atrial ventricular block'. This is not a valve blockage, but an electrical blockage; certain nerve impulses cannot make the heart beat properly. In fact, the cardiologist said the earlier 'fainting' episodes I'd described were not brain related, but had happened because of poor blood flow from the heart. In Brodie's case, the top half of his heart was beating, but the signal to make the lower half beat properly was absent. His resting heart rate should have been sixty to sixty-six beats per minute; his was much lower, at thirty-eight to forty-four.

At this news, my heart skipped a beat. It devastated me. Not only does this sweet lad have to deal with epilepsy, but he also has a heart condition? Not fair, God! I felt so helpless. There was not even a "bad news-good news" clause offered. No remarks such as "this is what he has, but this is how we'll treat it". There was nothing within their means they could do using medicine to correct or treat the heart. What the cardiologist could do, she said, was refer us to NC State Veterinary Hospital. There, they could put in a temporary pacemaker in order to get Brodie through the MRI, if I still wanted to pursue it.

I had to hit the pause button and think about that. Every waking moment, I prayed for courage and wisdom. Was it fair to Brodie to put him through all this, just to find the answer to what was or wasn't in his brain? Could that be done safely without risking his life? Was it practical to spend out even more money than I had already, to get the answers I was searching for? God, please give me your guidance. And what would I do if there was a brain tumor? Have it cut out? No, that was the one answer I knew. I would not put him through that. If this wasn't epilepsy, all we could do was to strive for the best quality of life for as much time as he may have. But in the end, I decided I had to know if I was dealing with epilepsy or something worse.

Not knowing would bring no quality of life or peace for either of us.

CHAPTER SIX

Cast thy burden upon the Lord and he shall sustain thee.
~Psalms 55:22a

The appointment at NC State Veterinary Hospital was scheduled for September 1- 2, 2015. We waited patiently, but nervously, in the lobby.

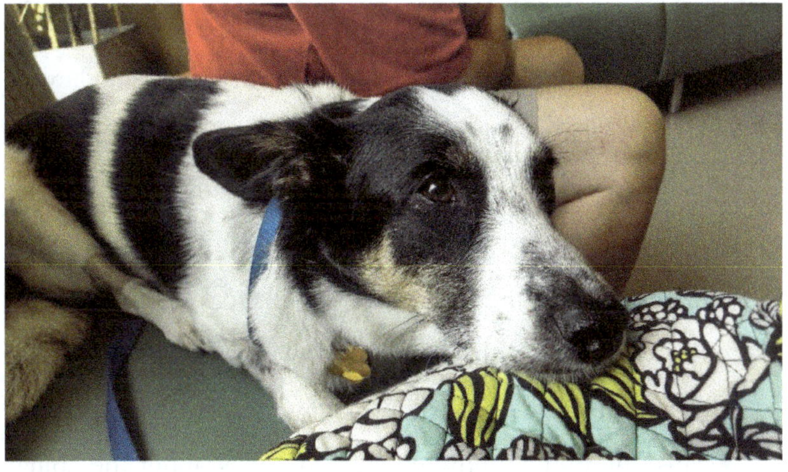

The first day was devoted to consultation, testing, reviewing results, and suggested recommendations. We met with a team of people: a 5th year student, a veterinary resident, and the attending veterinarian. Then, upon absorbing this knowledge and evaluating proposed options, it was my decision to move forward on the second day with treatment. Brodie's heart would be monitored carefully; a temporary pacemaker device would be inserted to get him through the procedure. A CT would be performed instead of an MRI, as the CT involves less sedation, lowering the risk to Brodie's heart. I don't recall there being any discussion around him possibly getting a permanent pacemaker; I didn't know enough to ask, nor was it suggested. The issue at hand was the CT, and how to best make it happen safely. They also said that it is standard to do a spinal tap when performing a diagnostic MRI or CT related to a brain issue, like epilepsy. I hadn't expected that and was frightened by it. They said examining the spinal fluid would help them rule out any bacterial infection that could contribute to the seizures, as well as give them more information if the CT didn't show anything suspicious. Because they knew how concerned I was about the spinal tap, they said if the CT images showed something bad, there would be no reason to pursue the tap. Not sure if that was any comfort, as then I'd be dealing with confirmation that his brain was diseased. But after absorbing the first day's results and advice, and considerable prayer overnight, on the second day, I agreed to the procedure, including the spinal tap. It seemed to me if I had come this far, I may as well go for the full diagnostic procedure. Brodie went to the back with the team of doctors, and I began what would be several hours of praying and waiting. In fact, not long after he went back, the student from the team came out and told me they could not insert the temporary pacemaker - the veins in his leg were too narrow to accommodate the wire. Instead, they would leave on the external pads to send an electrical pulse to his heart, much like the defibrillator pads used on humans. This was the rescue plan should Brodie experience any heart distress or failure. That nearly caused me some heart failure; my fear and anxiety shot up 100%! At that point, and not for the first time, I knew Brodie, and I were completely in God's hands. He would be the one to bring us through this, no matter what happened. I had a small Bible in my purse, and was reading some of my favorite verses, praying non-stop. I then ran across a verse that began to calm me: *The Lord is my light and salvation, whom shall I fear? The Lord is the strength of my life, of whom shall I be afraid? Psalms 27: 1*

I substituted "what" for "whom," and prayed (and paced) for the next hour or however long it was, waiting for word that Brodie was okay. I did not know if he would survive, but knew God was watching over us both, which helped to settle my fears. Finally, the student returned and said Brodie had made it through the CT and spinal tap just fine; they did not even have to use the pads at all to keep his heart beating. The good news too, was his brain did not have a tumor or any structural abnormality, so we were in the clear. His seizures were truly of epileptic origin, most likely because of genetics. The relief I felt was immeasurable. I was ever so glad to see Brodie and make the trip back home! I had no regrets about pursuing the CT, not just for the peace of mind it gave me concerning his epilepsy, but also for the revelation of his heart condition. Knowing Brodie's heart was not performing properly was clearly devastating and of great concern; but I never would have known about his heart condition had we not attempted the MRI.

We could manage Brodie's epilepsy with medicine, but his heart could not be treated. His resting heart rate was hovering around forty-two - forty-eight beats per minute.

The normal rate is a range of sixty to sixty-six beats per minute. A few weeks after the trip to NC State Veterinary Hospital, the local veterinary cardiologist performed another EKG and ultrasound of Brodie's heart; results were much the same as those in mid-August. She reported his heart was still normal in size, which was good (as a low heart rate over time will cause the heart to enlarge). I think I asked her if a permanent pacemaker would be a possibility for Brodie, but she said that was a selective process and few patients receive one. They rarely give one to a patient that already has a chronic condition or illness (like epilepsy?!). We continued him on a medication to help him breathe a little easier, but nothing could change his broken heart, nor mine. There were many times over the next couple of months that I wondered if he would just take one last breath and then be gone from me. I lived with that fear, but tried not to dwell on it. I trusted God had brought us through one ordeal safely, and was grateful for that. Even if Brodie's heart was compromised, we could still have good days ahead. Sadly, that thought was cut short about two months later.

CHAPTER SEVEN

No weapon that is formed against thee shall prosper.
~Isaiah 54:17

A couple of months after that trip to NC State Veterinary Hospital, I noticed a lump on Brodie's back between his shoulders. I thought it might be a "fatty tumor," which is a benign cyst. A lot of dogs have these; in fact, Brodie had one on his stomach that had been checked years earlier and found to be benign. I made an appointment for December 14, with the local veterinarian, to have this lump between his shoulders examined.

The doctors extracted fluid from the lump and examined it. I expected the next words to be "no worries, it is a benign cyst." To my dismay, it was a mast cell tumor - in other words, cancer. My entire world came to a stop. The fear and dread started rushing into my heart, my chest, my whole body. I was devastated. Not so much that it was a mast cell tumor. One of my previous dogs had had one of those. The veterinarian can remove those types of tumors safely. Rarely do they spread to other parts of the body if detected early, so I knew there was hope. My immediate thought, though, was that Brodie cannot withstand the surgery to have this removed; his heart won't take it and he will die on the table. What was I to do? If I didn't have the tumor removed, it would only continue to grow and spread throughout his body and eventually take his life. However, if removed in time, this type of cancer has a good recovery rate. The stumbling block was Brodie's heart problem. I even went as far to consult the cancer specialty veterinarian to see if there was a non-surgical option. She advised the protocol for a mast cell tumor is removal, followed by radiation or chemotherapy treatment as needed; however, those treatments are administered under anesthesia. In Brodie's case, even instead of surgery, treatment would require Brodie undergoing anesthesia; and his heart could not withstand that. It didn't take long for me to know our next step. Brodie and I had to return to NC State Veterinary Hospital. That very day, they submitted the referral paperwork for Brodie. I hoped and prayed God would work another miracle for my boy. We were very close to the holidays, and I knew we wouldn't get an appointment until

January. Those next few weeks were not festive for me. A heavy numbness settled over me that was hard to shake. I just wanted the holidays to pass quickly, so Brodie could get the help he needed. It was difficult to remain positive and not overthink what lay ahead. Those uncertain days taught me to truly live by faith and not by sight. Brodie's situation was seriously life threatening. I was extremely afraid and worried, and was not sure if Brodie's life could be saved. All I could do was pray and trust God to bring Brodie and me through it, knowing He is the way-maker.

CHAPTER EIGHT

I sought the Lord and he heard me and delivered me from all my fears. ~Psalms 34:4

On Tuesday, January 5, 2016, Brodie, and I, along with my dear friends Joan and Brad, traveled to the NC State Veterinary Hospital to see what could be done. During the two and one-half hour drive, it was hard not to wonder….. was I going to return from this trip with Brodie sitting beside me, alive and breathing? Or was I going to ride home with my boy in a body bag on the seat beside me? It was difficult, but I pushed that fear aside and put all trust in the One that was in control. We met with the surgery team that was assigned to Brodie and during introductions, the surgeon asked Joan and Brad their relation to me and Brodie. Joan's quick reply was, "we are his godparents!" All the doctors chuckled, but it was obvious they understood how special Brodie was to us. They spent the entire afternoon performing tests on Brodie (ultrasounds, EKG, etc.). About 4:30pm we got a call. The team was prepared to meet with us and discuss our available options.

We were presented with various safe scenarios for tumor removal by the surgeon and department lead in cardiology. The promising news was there was no evidence the cancer had spread to any other part of Brodie's body. All the tests and ultrasounds on his internal organs showed no cancer on his liver, stomach, spleen, lymph nodes, etc. However, the ultrasound on his heart and EKG showed the condition of his heart was worse than it had been during his visit the previous September. This was much more concerning to the cardiologist than the cancer issue. He considered the heart issue to be most life threatening. In fact, he said, "that tumor needs to be removed, yes; but we are going to address the heart issue first by giving Brodie a pacemaker!"

I couldn't believe my ears! Finally, an answer to many, many prayers was delivered. I knew the procedure would involve substantial risk, but it was also the miracle I had hoped for, one that would provide a genuine chance for Brodie to live a normal life (aside from his epilepsy). The doctors left the room for us to absorb what they proposed. The minute the door closed, Brad said, "that means the tumor is a Stage 2 or less...otherwise they would not consider giving Brodie a pacemaker." I knew that was true;

a pacemaker would not likely go to a dog who had advanced cancer and not expected to live much longer. Truly, hope was restored that cancer would not be the end of Brodie, and now neither would his failing heart. I was overjoyed, and grateful to God. I leaned in on His promise that what is meant for harm, He will turn it to good. (Genesis 50:20)

The doctors returned to the exam room; we agreed to move

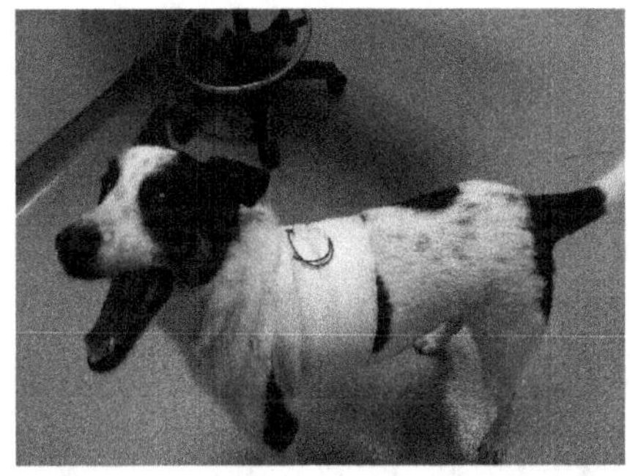

forward with the pacemaker procedure and made an appointment for two weeks later to have the tumor removed. My friends and I left Brodie in the capable care of the doctors; he would remain in the hospital with them until the day of his procedure. But the chief cardiologist instructed the vet technician to "put the pulse pads on him" until his surgery on Thursday, as a precaution. If Brodie's heart rate dropped too low or his heart stopped, they could quickly give him a shock to restart it.

I was glad to know they were taking precautions, but it unnerved me a little. Joan, Brad, and I returned to our hotel to freshen up and went in search of food. We asked directions to a local mall and found a restaurant that offered some variety. We enjoyed our meal, feeling relieved there was now a plan to deal with Brodie's issues. But I still thought about him during the meal and hoped he was fine. When we left the restaurant, we thought we were going back on the same road as we had taken to the mall, but discovered we missed a turn and were lost. Usually, I am good at finding my way, but it was dark, and I was not driving. It was the first week of January, and the sun sets at 5 pm, after all! I was getting more anxious, but tried not to show it. Worrying now that if the vet called to report Brodie was having an issue, we had no clue where or how quickly we could find our way back to the veterinary hospital. Thankfully, after stopping at a convenience store to ask for directions, we finally made it back to the hotel. I headed straight to bed, knowing the next day would be an anxious one as well.

CHAPTER NINE

*He healeth the broken in heart and bindeth up their
wounds. ~Psalms 147:3*

Sitting in the waiting room during the pacemaker procedure
was difficult to endure, but I trusted that all would go well.
The staff and doctors there always say, "no news is good
news," meaning that if you are not hearing from them, it
means surgery and procedures are proceeding according to
plan and there is no need to be concerned. Sounds good,
but it didn't keep me from worrying. Thankfully, my
friends were there for support, which was an immense help.
The doctors said pacemaker procedures can be tricky;
sometimes it goes quickly, and other times it takes longer,
to get the leads and wires inserted exactly where needed.
They promised they would not go past two hours of Brodie
being under anesthesia. They explained that being under
anesthesia for an extended time increases the potential risk
of infection and complications. Fortunately, after about an
hour and a half, the technician came out and said the
procedure was successful and they were ready to wake up

Brodie. They would keep him for an additional night of observation.

I was so overjoyed and relieved! I think I walked out of there on air. Still more mountains to climb, but at least a huge hurdle was behind us! We returned to the hotel to rest and pack, then came back for Brodie the next morning to start the drive home. Brodie was exhausted, as we all were, but it thrilled us to be reunited and ready to begin the journey home. They restricted him from jumping and running; he was to be on a leash every time he went outside. In fact, that day he started using a Halti leash, which goes around his nose and head, instead of a traditional collar around his neck. He could no longer have any pressure on his neck, as it would risk the pacemaker's leads coming loose. Brodie recovered nicely from the procedure, and I made sure we had quiet days and nights in order to help him heal and get his strength back.

CHAPTER TEN

Now the God of hope fill you with all joy and peace in believing. ~Romans 15:13

Approximately two weeks later, on January 21, 2016, we made a second trip to the NC State Veterinary Hospital to have the tumor removed. Again, Joan and Brad made the trip with Brodie and me. The drive up that Thursday was fine. It was a clear day; but a winter storm was approaching, and we knew it would begin before nightfall. We delivered Brodie to the hospital so he could settle in for the night, then we went for a quick dinner and returned to the hotel. When we woke the next morning, it was sleeting. Brad and I went over to the hospital's waiting room while Brodie had his surgery. Joan was not feeling well and remained at the hotel. The bad weather was a complication I could have done without. Although we had no trouble driving to the hospital, I wondered, did all the staff at the hospital make it into work? Was Brodie going to get the right level of care and expert treatment if the storm had created a staff shortage? I couldn't hide my fears and concerns, but the doctors and other staff assured me Brodie would absolutely get the expert care he deserved, no matter the weather. Sitting there in the waiting room was as nerve wrecking as before. It was so gray outside, sleet was pinging off the windows, and it seemed everything was in slow motion. Not sure if I remember the exact time his surgery was to begin, but they were late starting. So when I thought the procedure had begun, it had not. About the time I expected to get an update, I found they were just beginning! I think it was nearly noon or after when his surgery finally began. I knew Brodie was in expert hands, but every surgery has risk. They did not provide the updates with the usual frequency, which added to my worry. Because of the weather, the staff was moving through all the scheduled surgeries as quickly as they could. They focused on completing all the surgeries with no breaks in between, so they could let their personnel leave early; the roads were continuing to worsen. It was a situation requiring more patience and calm than I had on my own. I kept reading my Bible to stay in God's word and presence. It was not until about 2pm that the surgeon came to the waiting room to let us know that Brodie's surgery was over and he was doing fine. At that point, I finally could breathe normally again. I felt waves of relief wash over me, removing all the worry and fear from the previous hours. Brodie had survived the surgery!

The surgeon said he had made about a ten to twelve inch incision in order to be sure he removed the entire tumor and some additional underlying tissue. I would get a full pathology report later, but at that point, I was just grateful the surgery went as expected, and Brodie was resting well. He obviously would be in recovery overnight; the doctors recommended keeping Brodie a second night so they could monitor and keep him comfortable. Given the icy road conditions, we could not depart for home until Sunday anyway, so Brodie having an extra night to recover was the perfect arrangement. Knowing Brodie was in excellent hands, Brad and I left the hospital to return to the hotel. We found a convenience store that was still open and loaded up on snacks and whatever goodies we could find to finish waiting out the storm. I got a phone update on Saturday morning and was told Brodie was recovering very well.

On Sunday morning, we went to the Emergency entrance of the Vet Hospital to pick up Brodie. He was rather pitiful looking, with that long incision on his back, all swollen and red, but I was so glad to see him! After going over his discharge instructions, Joan and I loaded Brodie into my car, and Brad followed behind us as we started the long trip home. We had traveled a few miles down the beltway, and then took the exit to highway 64 West. The roads were not clear, but passable, so we were going slowly. At the end of the ramp, the stoplight caught us. I was sitting in the back seat with Brodie, and Joan was driving my car. Brad was following behind us in theirs. Suddenly, she said, "oh my goodness, Brad just got rear-ended!" Sure enough, the car behind Brad on the ramp had hit a patch of ice, lost traction, and plowed right into the back of his vehicle. Fortunately, no one was injured, but the police were called to investigate. Joan stayed with Brad, and I drove my car up to the next exit to wait for them. Of all things to happen, when all any of us wanted was to get Brodie back home safely. Thankfully, it didn't take too long for them to catch up with me after they filed the police report. We were just grateful there was minor damage to their car and none that rendered it undrivable. Joan again got in to drive my car, and I sat in the back seat with Brodie, with Brad following in his vehicle. We made it all the way home without further incident. After two surgeries in one month, we were exhausted and very relieved to have successfully survived it all. Now we hopefully waited for good news concerning the pathology report.

CHAPTER ELEVEN

...I am the Lord that healeth thee. ~Exodus 15:26b

Brodie and I both were glad to be home! For the next several days, he took pain medicine and muscle relaxers, plus every two hours I put an ice pack on his neck for ten minutes to help reduce the swelling. Turns out, a bag of frozen vegetables makes an excellent ice pack!

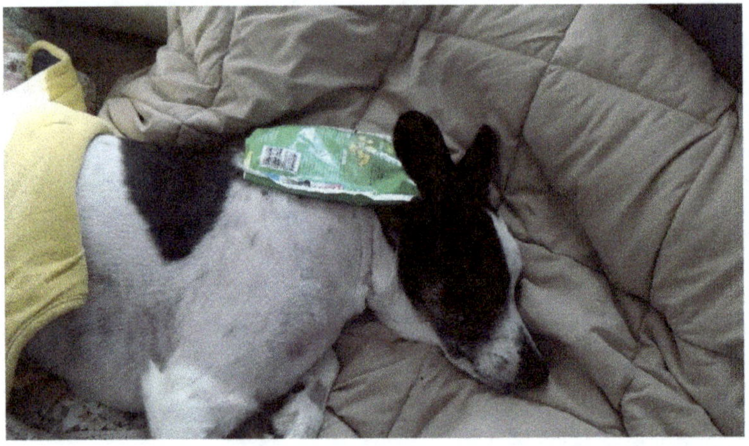

He tolerated the ice pack therapy well and was great at taking his medicine. Since they had shaved his neck and back, he needed to stay covered. With January being a cold weather month, I kept his doggie "coat" on him to provide warmth, even inside the house.

His neck was so stiff I put his food and water bowl up on a stool, so he wouldn't have to bend his head to eat or drink. He had one seizure during that time, on the first full day we were home. I think all that he had been through caught up with him, but it was a brief seizure. Probably the lingering anesthesia in his system helped minimize the severity and duration, which was a blessing. The thrashing in a full seizure could have possibly pulled open his stitches, but thankfully, that didn't happen. A few days after we were home, I had a call from the vet to give me results of the pathology report. It was very encouraging! They confirmed it was a low Grade II tumor, and they had no reason to believe that the cancer would return anywhere else in his body. No radiation or chemotherapy was recommended either, which was also good news. Once again, God had blessed us with the best possible outcome!

Overall, Brodie's recovery went very well; in time, his incision healed, and he returned to his normal activities. Within approximately three months, Brodie had regained his strength, and the incision had healed nicely.

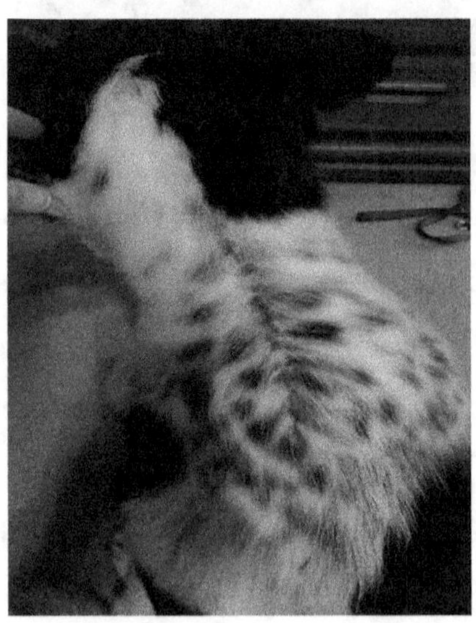

He became his playful self again, enjoying just "being a dog." It was such a relief to see him run and play freely, knowing his heart and body were now whole and healed. In April 2016, Brodie had a return visit to NC State Veterinary Hospital for a recheck of his pacemaker. Everything was working well; future pacemaker rechecks would now be performed only once a year.

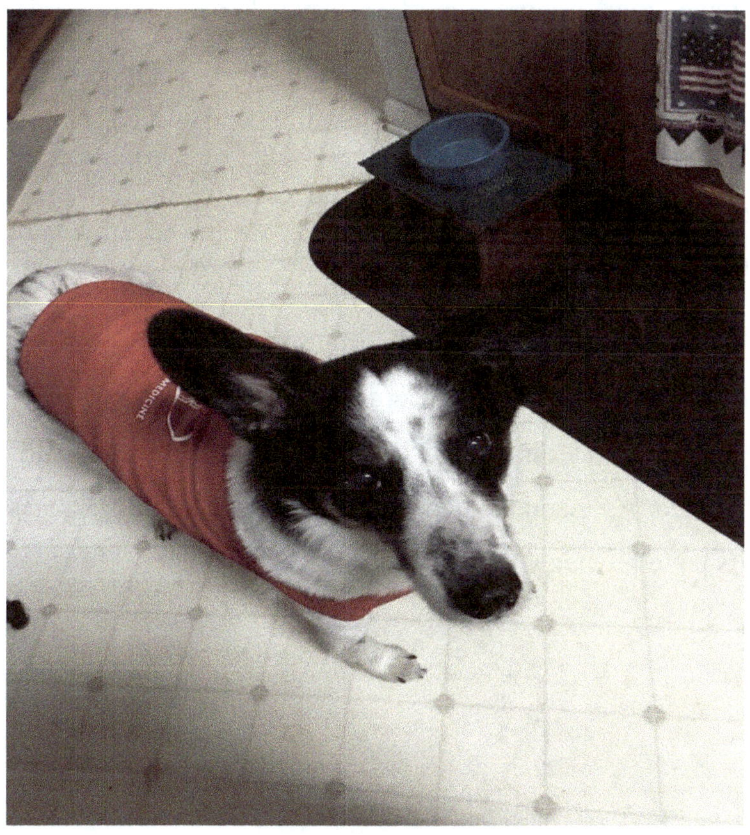

It was a joy and a blessing for Brodie to have his heart working properly and the cancer was no longer an issue; but we continued to live with the epilepsy. Later that spring, on April 25, 2016, Brodie had another grand mal seizure. In fact, over that next year, he continued to have seizures about every two to three months. Some of these were also cluster episodes. In May 2017, he had a bad grand mal seizure, and for several days afterwards, continued to have focal seizures. They added another medicine, Keppra. It, combined with his other medications, finally gave us the control over seizures that had eluded us for so long. In fact, once this change was made, Brodie did not have another grand mal seizure for many years. He only experienced the occasional focal seizure. This control is possible, but not always common, with epilepsy patients. We were grateful for this blessing, but did not take it for granted. As mentioned earlier, epilepsy sometimes changes its pattern when you least expect it.

Happy
14th Birthday
to
Brodie!

CHAPTER TWELVE

...ye thought evil against me, but God meant it unto good.
~Genesis 50:20

Living with canine epilepsy is difficult. It is an uncertain path, with many difficulties. It takes persistence in finding the right combination of medications and other treatments that will provide management of the disease, and enable your pet to maintain a good quality of life. Ironically, Brodie's epilepsy saved his life. Without searching for the cause of his seizures, I would not have known Brodie had a heart condition; one that could not be treated with medication or corrected without surgery. I am not sure how long Brodie would have been able to live with a heart that was not functioning properly, perhaps only months. When they delivered the cancer diagnosis, it devastated me, and I thought it would surely end his life. Instead, it led to the decision of Brodie receiving a pacemaker to correct his heart. Brodie's heart was then strong enough to undergo surgery, and the doctors removed the cancer successfully. Each of these conditions could have ended Brodie's life, but I learned not all bad things end badly. Before this experience, I had heard it said that "what is meant to harm you, God will work unto good." That was certainly true for Brodie and me! When I look back at how these events unfolded, I am humbled to know God had his hand on me and Brodie the whole time. Before I ever attempted the MRI, God already had the pacemaker lined up; and once in place, then a successful surgery that saved Brodie's life. All of His handiwork knitted these events into a beautiful conclusion. Each hurdle, every challenge, the anguish, and tough decisions - all were the stepping stones on this journey - a journey sustained through faith and with hope.

Epilogue

After the last grand mal seizure in 2017, Brodie never had another major seizure. His pacemaker was checked every year, and it continued to perform well throughout the rest of his days. In the latter part of his life, Brodie had many happy and fun days - living his best life as a normal dog: seizure free, cancer free, and "young at heart." Sadly, Brodie passed away February 24, 2022, at 14 years, 9 months. It was not because of epilepsy–he remained victorious over that! Nor was it because of any heart related issue–his pacemaker never failed. He died from vestibular syndrome, brought on by a brain tumor that likely developed in his last year of life.

Brodie and I had a remarkable life together, and he fought the good fight right until the end. To say I am heartbroken and devastated does not describe the depth of my loss. Yet I am grateful that God sent Brodie to me, and equipped me to give him the healthiest life I could, despite all the challenges. I am thankful for all the years I had with

Brodie, but especially for the six extra ones made possible by God's grace and mercy–all filled with love and hope! Brodie's journey has ended. He is at rest; but he remains in my heart forever, reminding me daily of God's goodness and faithfulness.

Memorial Brick at NC State Veterinary Hospital

PROCEEDS STATEMENT

Net proceeds from this book are donated to Brodie's Endowment for Epilepsy Research, through NC State Veterinary Medical Foundation. Its two-fold mission:

1) to fund research on the causes and enhance future treatments;
2) to provide educational outreach and support for families whose beloved dogs are living with this illness.

ACKNOWLEDGMENTS

Thank you to my family and friends for being on this journey with Brodie and me. Your love and support have been invaluable.

Special thanks go to my friend Jane Hyer and her husband Bud for being my "boots on the ground" during the two trips to NC State Veterinary Hospital. Jane passed away in 2019, but I know she is watching over me and keeping an eye on Brodie.

Thank you, Darla Clark Allred, for your amazing portrait of my Brodie that became the book cover. Not only is it a perfect likeness of him, but you also captured his enduring spirit. Please visit Darla's website, www.petportraitsbydarla.com, or find it under the same name on Facebook.

I particularly want to thank all the veterinarians that assisted and partnered with me in providing Brodie's medical care. You enabled me to give him the best life possible for fourteen years. No words can adequately express my immense gratitude.

Dr. Ashley Gray, DVM- formerly of Animal Medical Hospital, Charlotte, NC; currently Medical Director of Veterinarian Emergency Group, Charlotte, NC.

Dr. Sandy Tisdelle -DVM - Animal Medical Hospital, Charlotte, NC

Dr. Russell Quigley -DVM, DACVIM (Neurology), Carolina Veterinary Specialists, Matthews, NC

Dr. Elizabeth Cox - DVM, DACVIM (Cardiology), Carolina Veterinary Specialists, Matthews, NC

Dr. Karen Munana -DVM, MS, DACVIM (Neurology), NC State College of Veterinary Medicine

Julie Nettifee - MS, RVT, VTS (Neurology), NC State College of Veterinary Medicine

Dr. Bruce Keene -DACVIM (Cardiology), NC State College of Veterinary Medicine

Dr. Teresa DeFrancesco-DACVIM, Diplomate, American College of Veterinary Emergency and Critical Care, NC State College of Veterinary Medicine

These veterinarians treated Brodie at NC State Veterinary hospital in 2016, but now work elsewhere:

Dr. Christopher Adin–Diplomate, American College of Veterinary Surgeons

Dr. Darcy Adin–DVM, DCVIM, (Cardiology)

Dr. Kate Woodruff, DVM, (Cardiology)

Dr. Akshaya Maller, DVM, (Soft Tissue Surgery)

About the Author

 Hope Anderson has lived in Charlotte, NC her entire life and had many family dogs growing up. As an adult, her continued love of dogs led to her becoming a 'dog mom' to her first Golden Retriever, Treasure. Hope was also active for many years in the Charlotte branch of Golden Retriever Rescue, helping to re-home unwanted or abandoned Golden Retrievers into new, forever homes. Two of those rescues found a home with her, Sassy, and then Hannah. Each of her "Golden girls" deeply impacted her life in their own way; but needing a change, her next dog was a male Border Collie mix named Brodie. Hope graduated from UNC-Charlotte with a BA in Psychology. Her career years were with corporate companies in technology and banking industries. Retired as of September 2021, she enjoys her church activities and occasional trips to the North Carolina beaches or mountains.

CANINE EPILEPSY RESOURCE LIST

Canine epilepsy veterinary diagnosis and treatment
International Epilepsy Task Force Consensus Reports
 www.biomedcentral.com/collections/ivetf

ACVIM Consensus Statement
http://onlinelibrary.wiley.com
(in search field type canine epilepsy to generate list of reports)

Clinical studies in canine epilepsy & cancer
NC State canine epilepsy studies
http://go.ncsu.edu/epilepsyresearch

Nationwide AVMA clinical studies database
https://ebusiness.avma.org

Veterinary cancer trials
www.vetcancersociety.org/pet-owners/clinical-trials

Canine Epilepsy Support
-   On Facebook -
Canine Epilepsy
Dogs with Epilepsy
The Wally Foundation-canine epilepsy

- Websites -
Canine Epilepsy Resource Center & Epil-K9 List
www.canine-epilepsy.com

Canine Epilepsy Support Group
https://www.canineepilepsysupport.co.uk

Caring for the caregiver
Resources in self compassion, Dr. Kristin Neff
 http://self-compassion.org

-Apps-
Smiling Mind (free)
Calm (free trial)
Headspace (14-day free trial)

www.ingramcontent.com/pod-product-compliance
Lightning Source LLC
Chambersburg PA
CBHW050604160726
48003CB00003B/1042